Why aren't ghosts good at lying?

You can always see right through them.

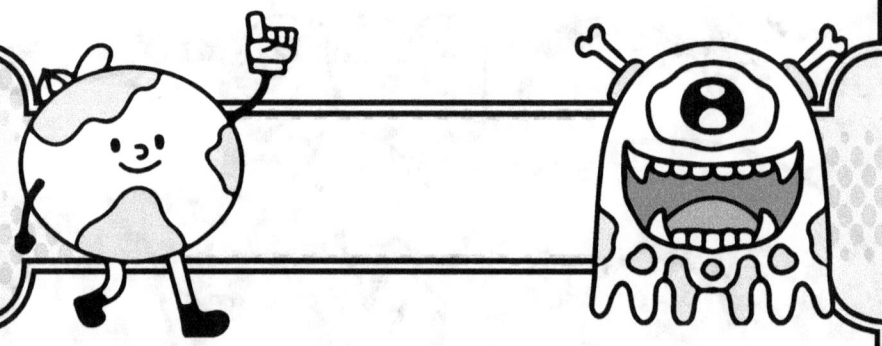

What could you call two apes that share an Amazon account.

Prime-mates.

During which season do people get injured the most?

The fall.

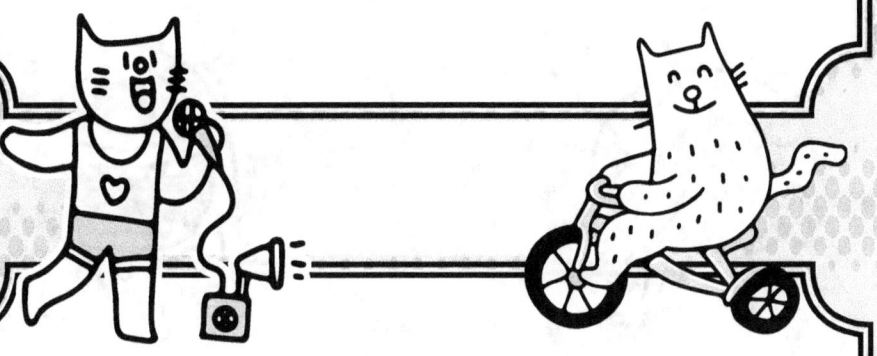

How did Mr Candle ask Ms Candle for a date?

Will you go out with me?

Why is an elephant's skin so wrinkly?

Well, have you ever tried to iron one?

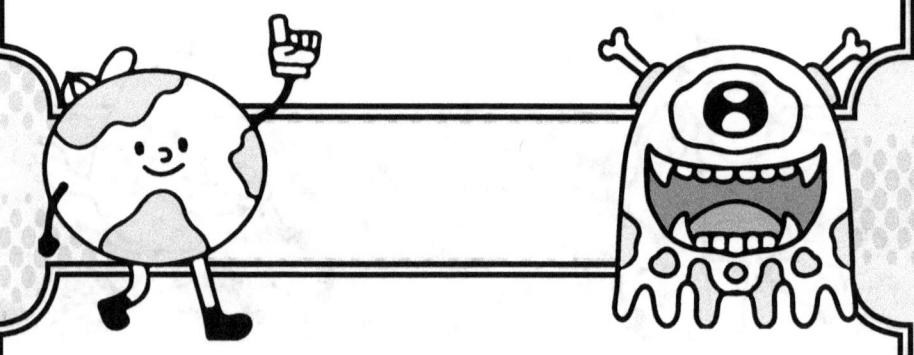

Who won the race between all the princesses?

Rapunzel, by a hair.

Which bird usually wears a wig?

A bald eagle.

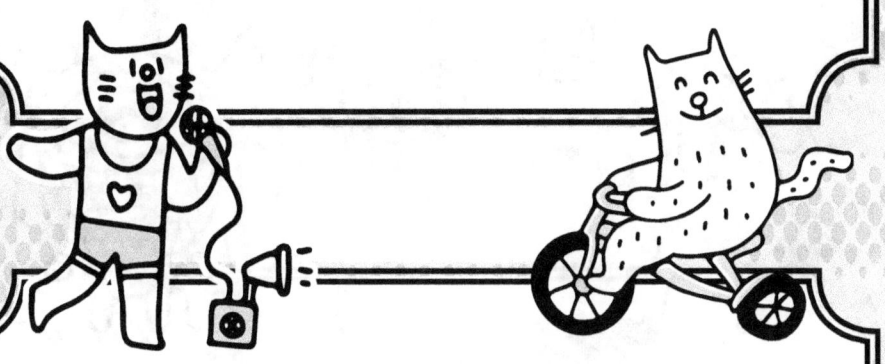

How are false teeth the same as the moon?

They both come out at night.

Where do monkeys go if they lose their tale?

They go back to the re-tailer.

What do cats use to defend their territory?

Cat-apults.

Why did the phone have to walk through the water?

It was wading for a phone call.

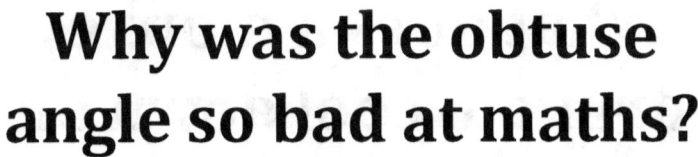

Why was the obtuse angle so bad at maths?

Because he was never right.

Why is the Christmas alphabet different to the regular alphabet?

The Christmas alphabet has Noel.

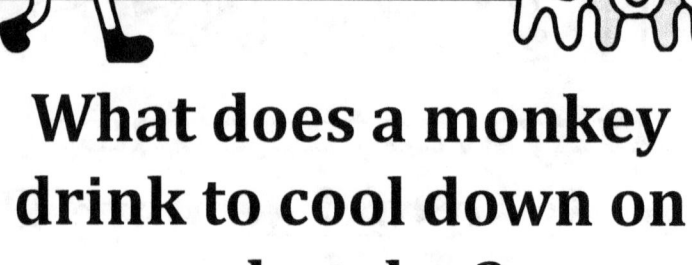

What does a monkey drink to cool down on a hot day?

Iced Chimpan-tea.

What part of your face can bring the world to an end?

Your apoca-lips.

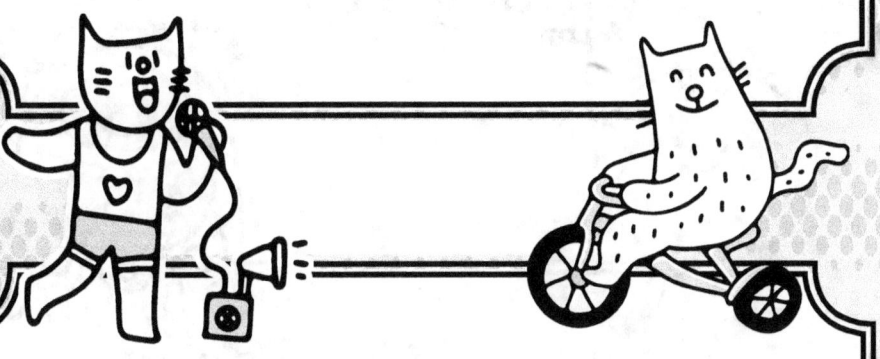

Which candy is a Christmas tree's favorite?

Orna-mints.

How hot do you think it was during that math class on angles?

I checked - it was 90 degrees.

What did the doctor recommend to add whole grain to the monkey's diet?

Bran-anas.

Why do aliens find it hard to concentrate in class?

They always get spaced out.

When is the best time to have a dentist appointment?

Tooth-hurty.

What did the pharaoh write at the start of all his letters?

Tomb it may concern!

What would you get when a cow refuses to be milked?

Udder chaos.

When is a door not just a door?

When it is ajar.

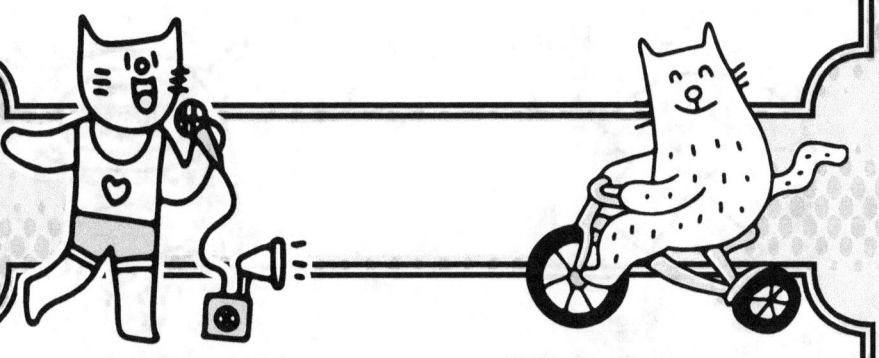

What's the difference between a healthy rabbit and a comedy rabbit?

One's a fit bunny, the other's a bit funny.

What is the name of a man who has a large flat fish on his head?

Ray.

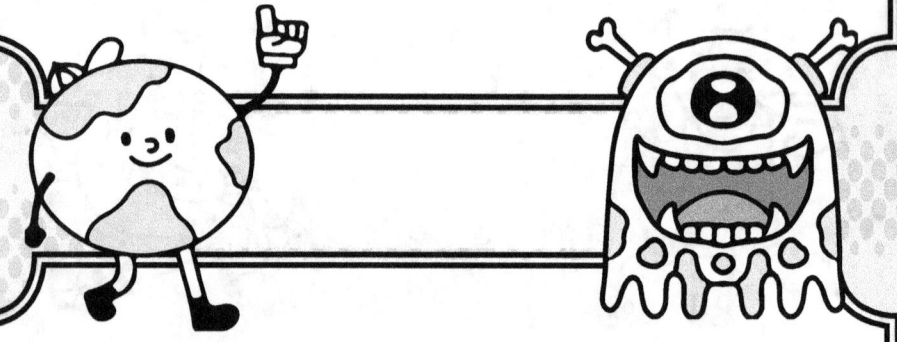

Why should nobody trust Scar?

Because he's always lion.

Where does ice cream go when it graduates high school?

Cool-ege.

How can you fit more pigs on your farm?

Just build a sty-scraper.

What would you get when you mix a snowperson with a vampire?

Frost-bite.

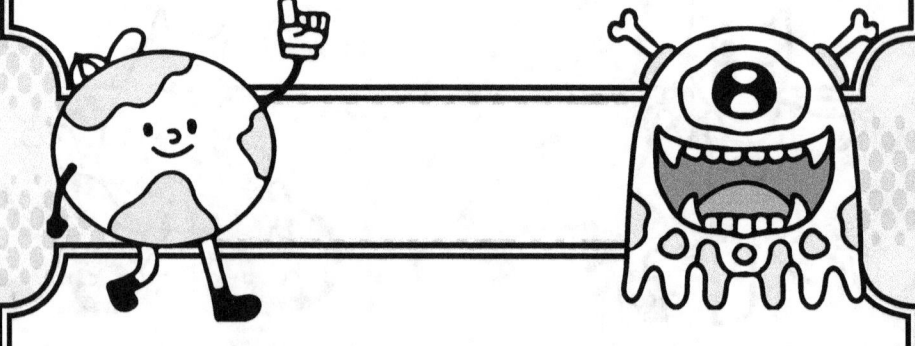

Why can't polar bears eat Penguins?

They can never get the wrappers off.

Why can't skunks afford expensive dinners?

Because they only have one scent.

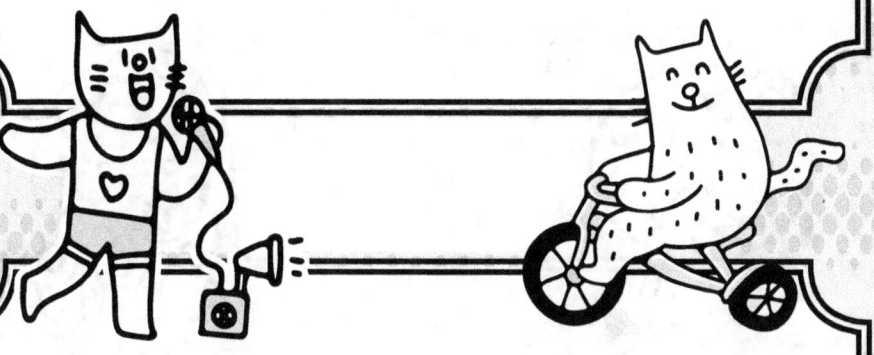

How do reindeers know when it's Christmas?

They just look at their calen-deer.

I think my pet bunny enjoyed the action movie.

He found it totally hare-raising.

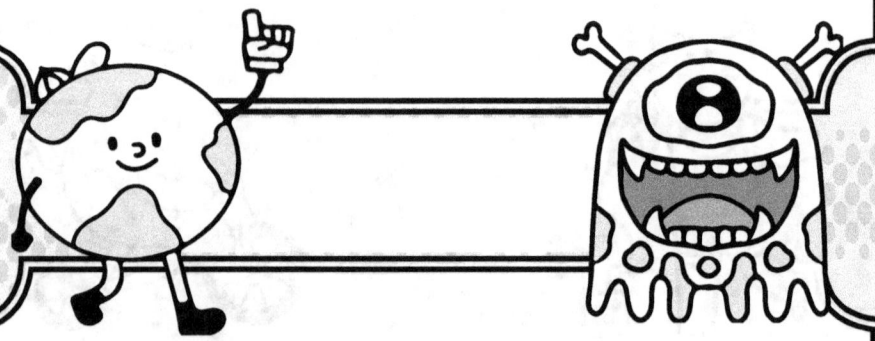

What do llamas get when they graduate from high school?

A high school dip-llama.

How much does a pirate pay to get his ears pierced?

About a buck-an-ear.

What did the dinner plate say to the utensils?

Dinner is on me.

Which part of skydiving is the hardest?

The ground below.

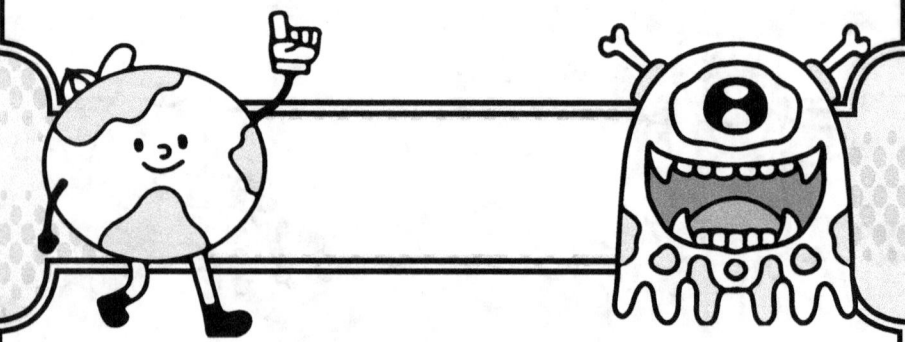

Why did the professor wear shades during class?

Because her students were so bright.

Knock, knock.
Who's there?
Amarillo.
Amarillo who?
Amarillo nice once you get to know me.

Which kind of roads do ghosts like to walk down?

Dead ends.

What happened to the two thieves who stole a calendar?

They each got six months.

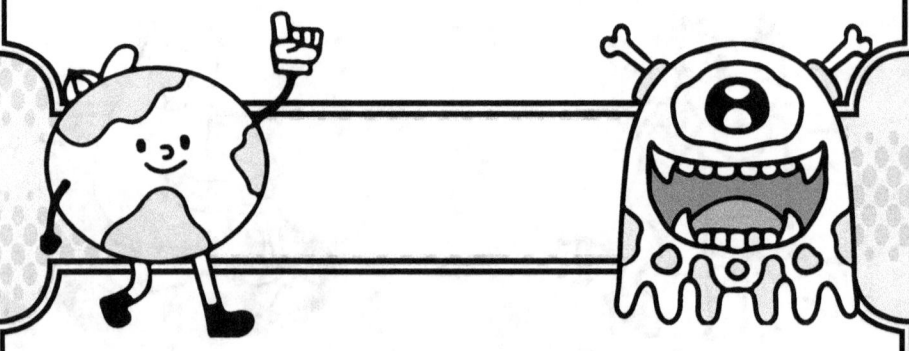

Where do dads keep all of their jokes?

In the dadabase.

Why did the teacher bring a math paper into the pool?

She wanted to test the water.

What should you call a shark that writes famous plays?

William Shark-speare.

Why did the tortoise have to get a new cell phone?

Because she filled her old one with shellfies.

What is the most popular seafood for monkeys?

Shrimp-anzee.

What do they call it when a cat wins a dog-grooming show?

cat-has-trophy.

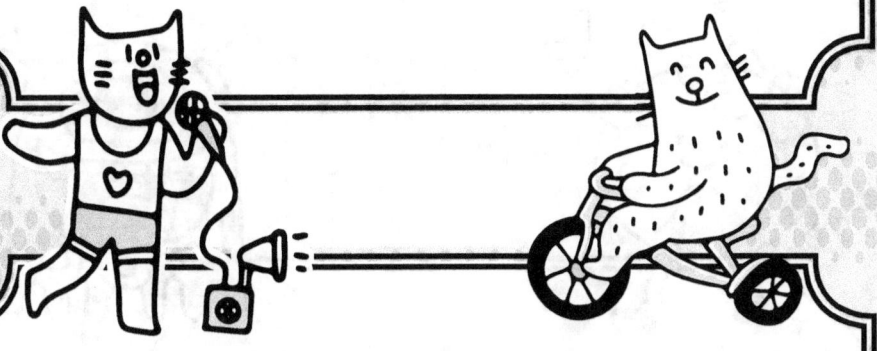

My mom asked my dad if he'd seen the dog bowl.

He said he didn't know that our dog liked bowling.

Why is popcorn so popular in the army?

Because it has lots of kernels.

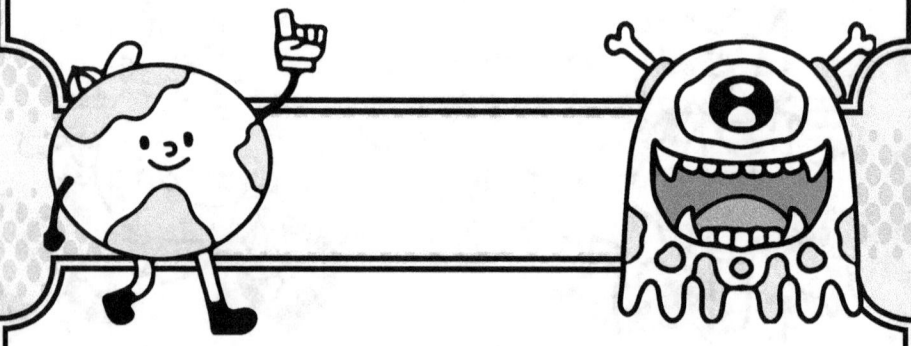

What happens when the Queen burps?

She issues a royal pardon.

What does a snowman take when it gets too hot?

A chill pill.

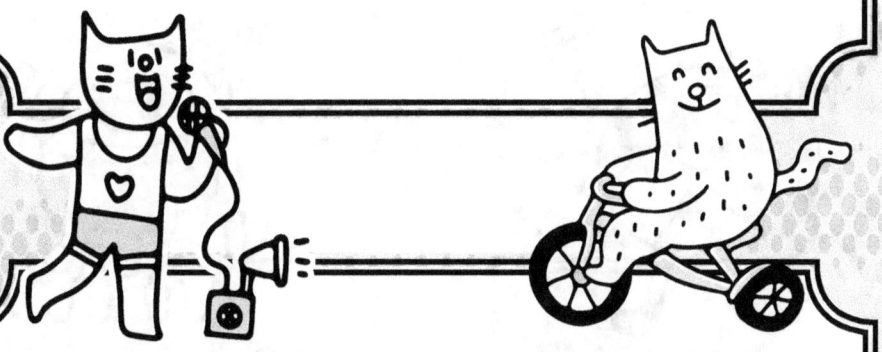

I was worried about the man who got hit in the head with a Pepsi can.

Lucky for him it was a soft drink.

Where is the most popular holiday destination for cows?

Moo Zealand.

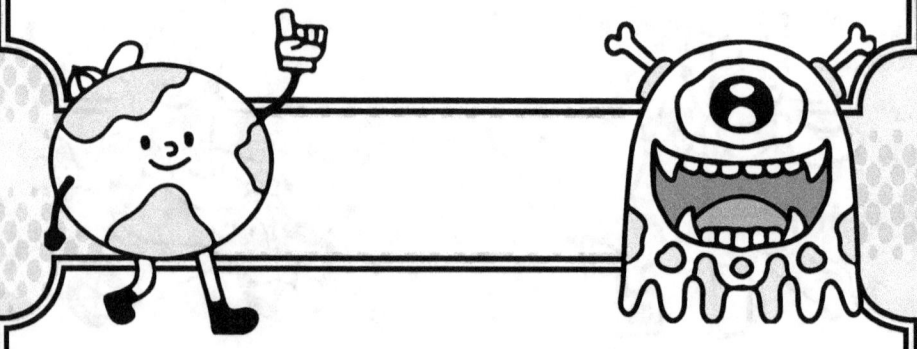

Why did the bicycle need to lie down?

It was feeling two-tired.

When do most astronauts eat lunch?

At launch time.

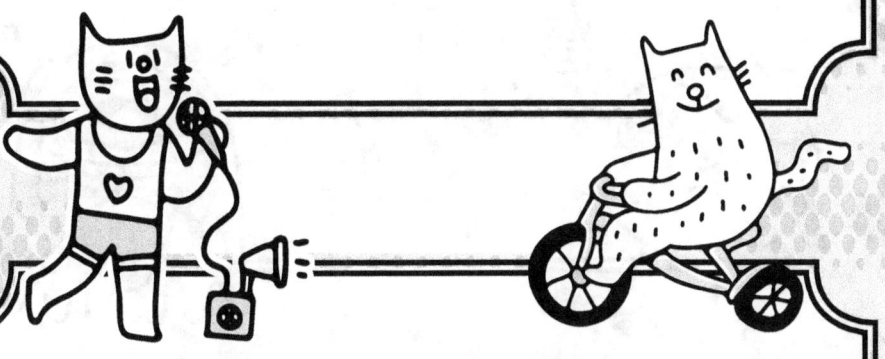

How did the owl feel when he lost his voice?

He couldn't give a hoot.

Why did the old man fall down a well?

He could not see that well.

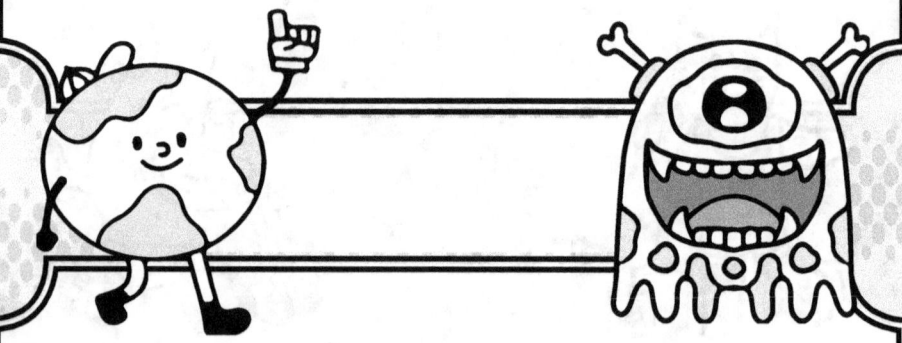

What would you say to a mountain that told really funny jokes?

You're hill-arious.

What would a llama say if a giant asteroid was about to collide with Earth?

It's llamageddon!

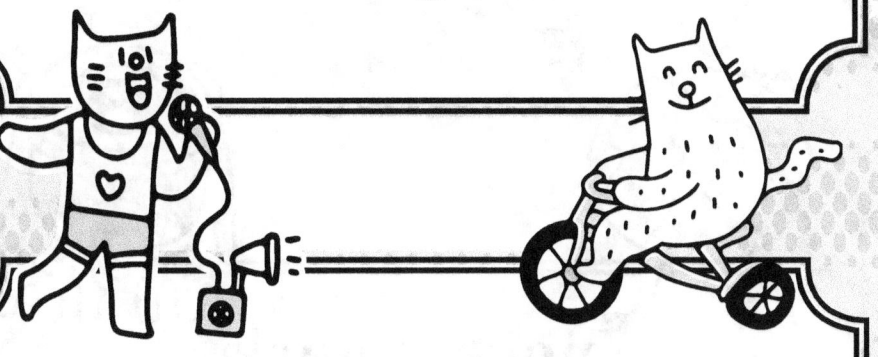

What sort of music do Santa's elves listen to?

Wrap music.

How can you make gold soup easily?

Just make sure to use 14 carrots.

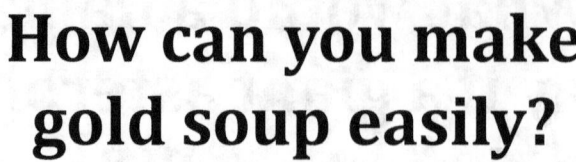

Knock, knock.
Who's there?
A mustache.
A mustache who?
A mustache you a question, but I'll shave it until later!

What do they call people who only eat popcorn?

Corn-ivores.

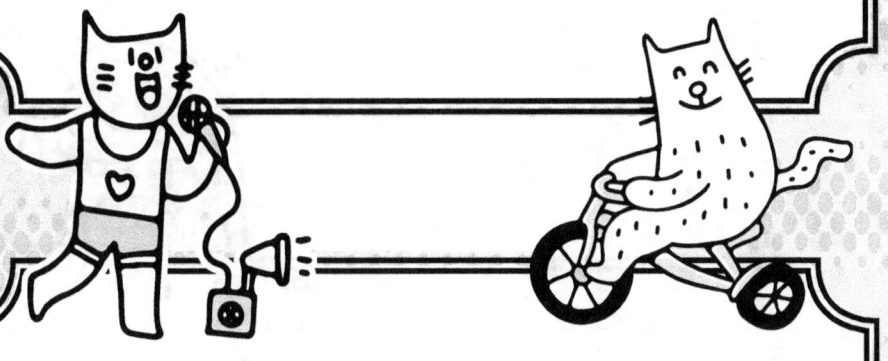

What can fall but never hits the ground?

The temperature.

What always comes at the end of each Christmas Day?

The letter Y.

What do baby computers call their fathers?

Data.

Which famous composer do most llamas listen to?

Wolfgang Llamadeus Mozart.

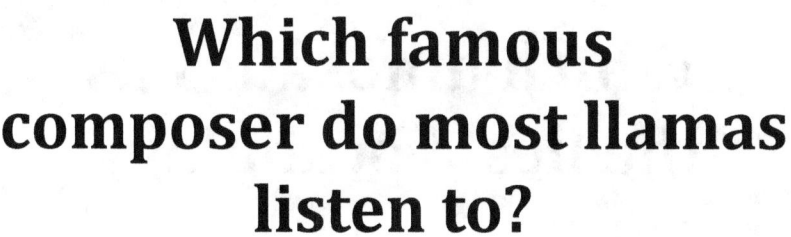

What drink do trees enjoy the most?

Root beer.

Which dinosaur has the best vocabulary?

The thesaurus.

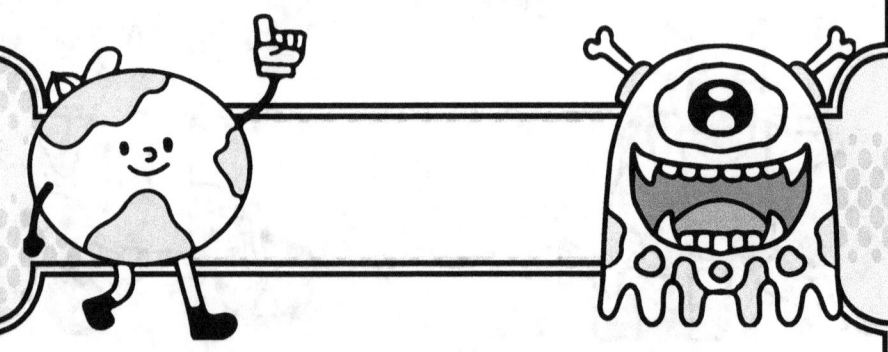

Why did they put the chef in prison?

He beats eggs and whipped cream.

You have me with your meals but never eat me. What am I?

Cutlery.

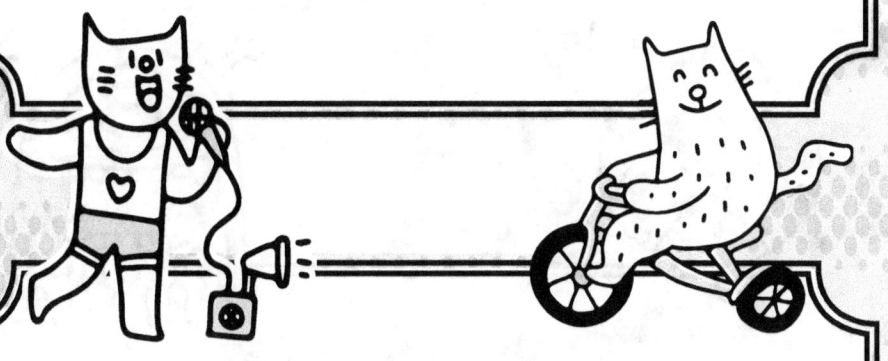

Why did the frog have to get the bus to work?

Her car got toad away.

What do rabbits do to stay fit?

Hare-robic exercise.

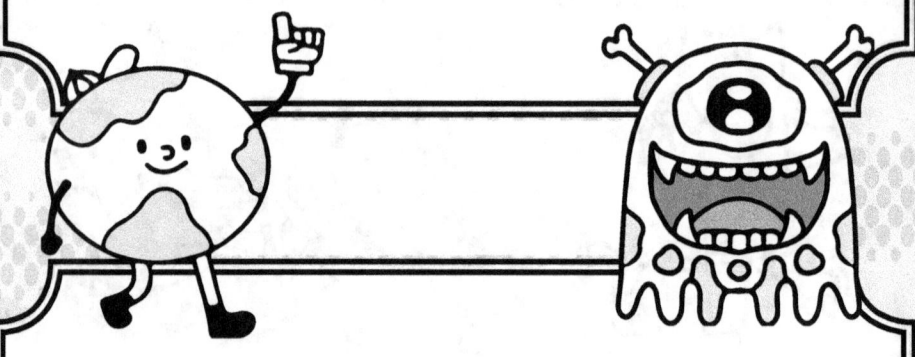

What Mexican food do cats love?

A purr-itos.

What should you do if an oyster gets sick?

Call a clam-bulance immediately.

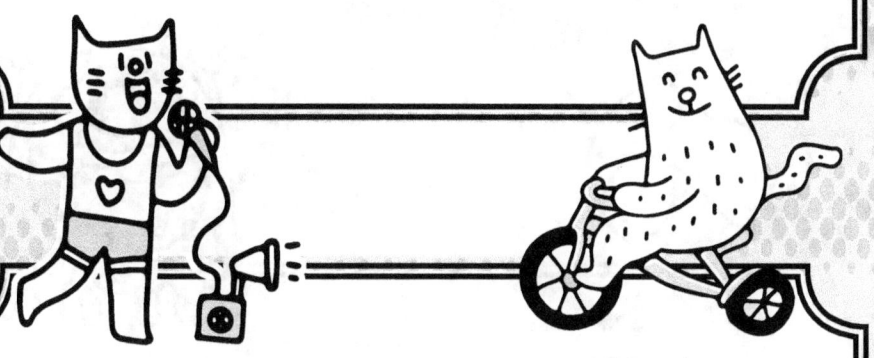

What happens if you wear a snow suit indoors?

It melts all over your carpet.

Why shouldn't you eat Christmas decorations?

You'll get tinselitus.

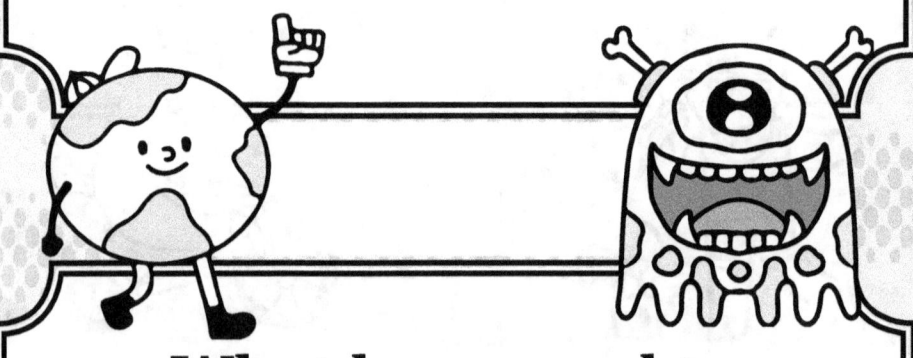

What happened to the rancher who had 98 cows in his field?

After rounding them up, he had 100.

What happens if you cross a llama and a sweet potato?

You get a yyama.

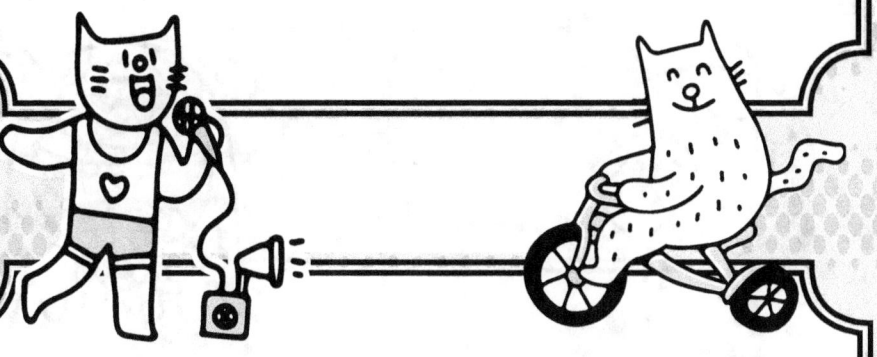

When do Oreos need to visit the dentist?

When they lose their filling.

What happened when the past, present and future were in the same room?

It got pretty tense.

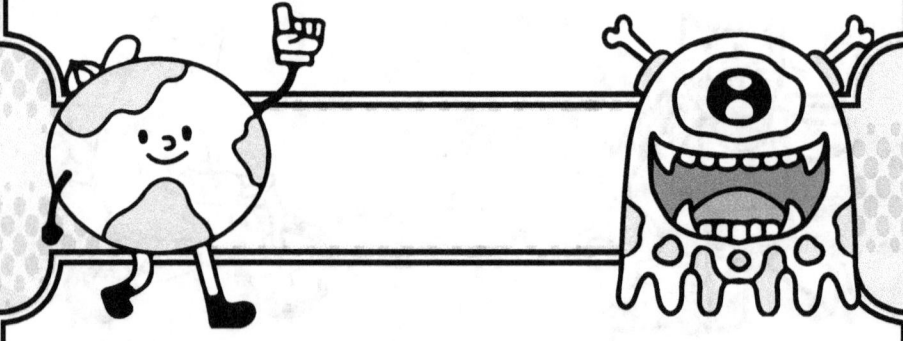

Which nation do teachers visit over and over again?

Expla-nation.

What did the pear say when it saw a shoeless man?

You look like you need a pair of shoes.

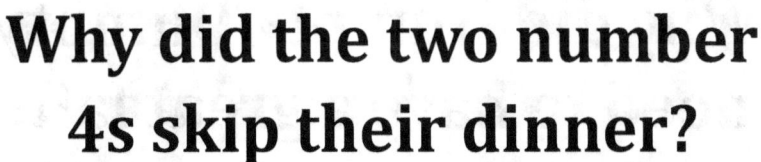

Why did the two number 4s skip their dinner?

They already 8.

What made the PowerPoint cross the road?

It wanted to get to the other slide.

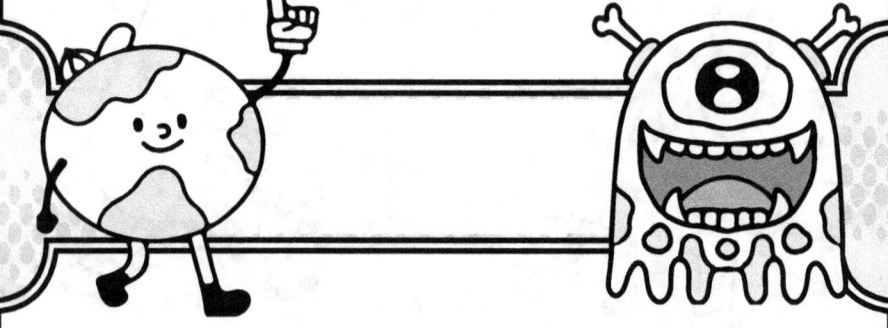

Why did Humpty Dumpty need to have a great fall?

Because he'd had quite a miserable summer.

Why did the computer feel cold?

It left too many windows open.

What did the monkey say after the tiger grabbed him by the tail?

Well, that's the end of me!

Why doesn't peanut butter tell anyone its secret?

It's afraid that people will spread it.

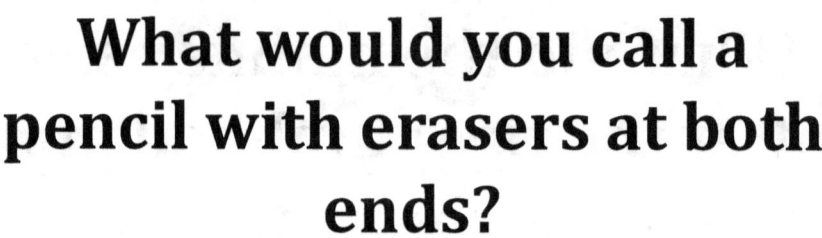

What would you call a pencil with erasers at both ends?

Totally pointless.

What do they say when a person gets stuck between two llamas?

They got llamanated.

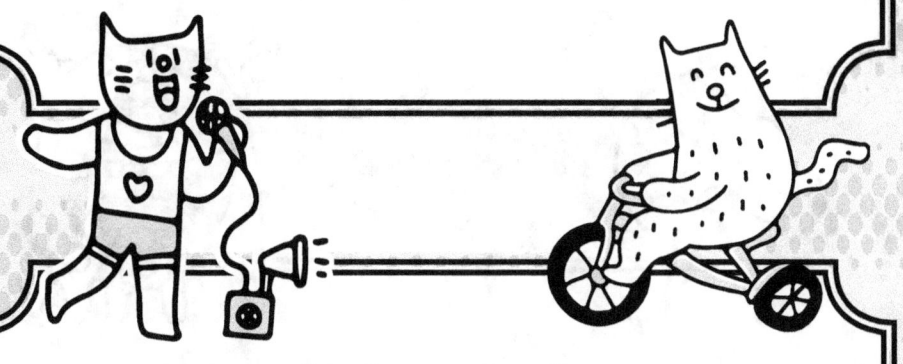

How did Nala locate Simba when he got lost?

By following his foot prince.

What could you call a bunny with lots of money?

A million-hare.

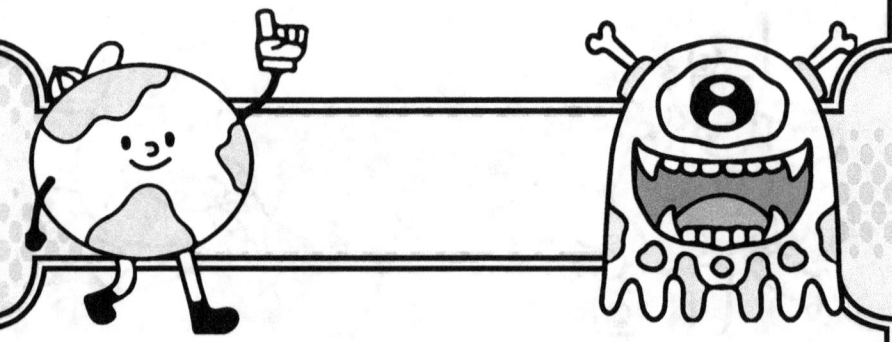

Why did they find cheese next to the computer?

The mouse had had a little a snack.

How is an injured lion different to a wet day?

One roars with pain and the other pours with rain!

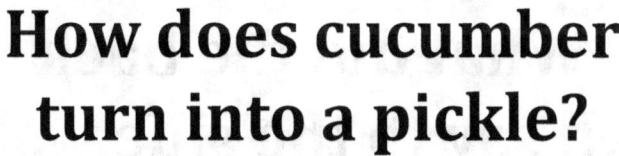

How does cucumber turn into a pickle?

It has to endure a jarring experience.

I cannot walk, but I have legs. What am I?

A table.

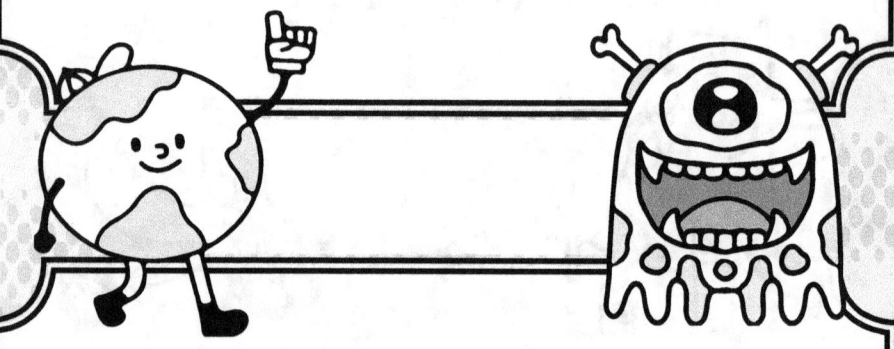

What did the back wall say to the side wall?

Let's meet at the corner!

What do llamas drink to cool down on hot days?

Llama-nade.

Where should rats go when they have toothache?

To see the rodent-ist.

Which US president did most llamas vote for?

Barack Ollama.

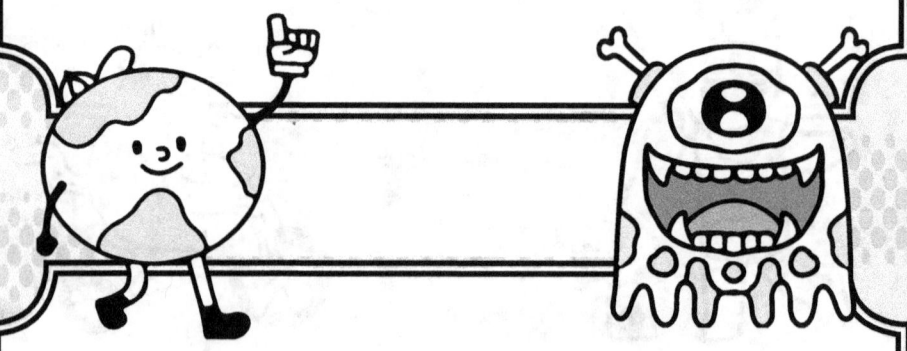

What made it get so hot in the stadium after the baseball game?

All of the fans left.

What would you get if you mix a cow and a chicken?

Roost beef.

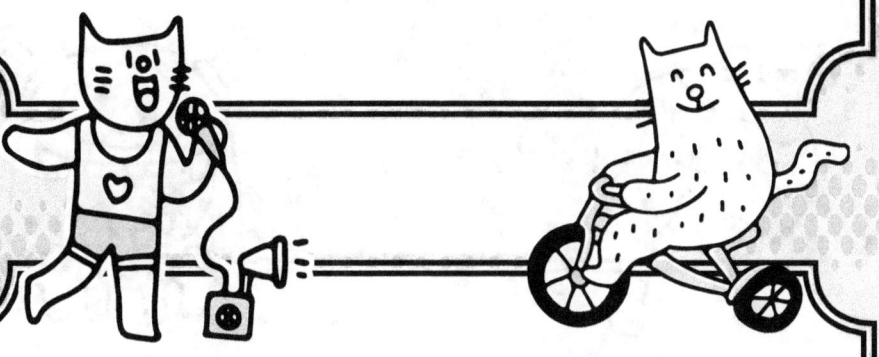

What sort of snake can you find on your car?

A windshield viper.

Did you hear about that uncle who drank 8 sodas?

He burped 7UP.

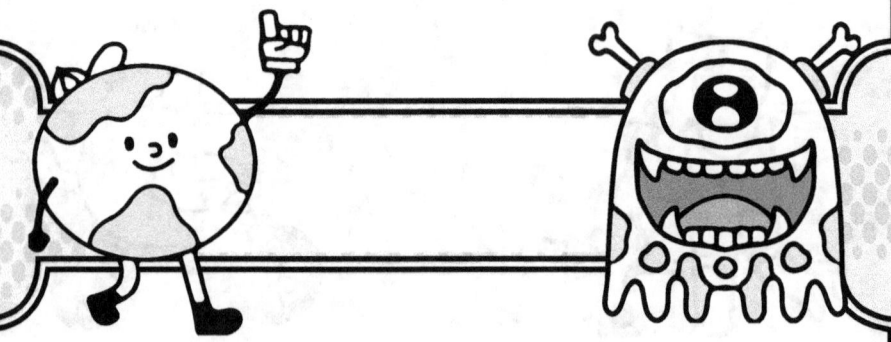

Why was the ornithologist showing off?

He was being a know-it-owl.

Why shouldn't you wait for Peter Pan at the airport?

He usually Neverlands on time.

How do the Malfoy family get into bed each night?

They Slytherin.

Why can't pirates learn the alphabet very quickly?

They often spend years at C.

Why didn't the Dalmatian have any dessert?

Dinner already hit the spots.

What do they call a knight that doesn't like fighting?

Sir Render.

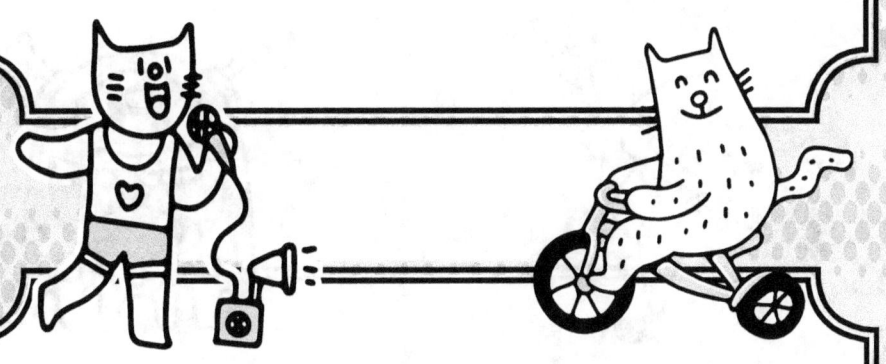

How do you know if an owl is angry with you?

Because it will sc-owl at you.

Why didn't Timon want to hang around with Pumbaa any more?

He was being too boar-ing.

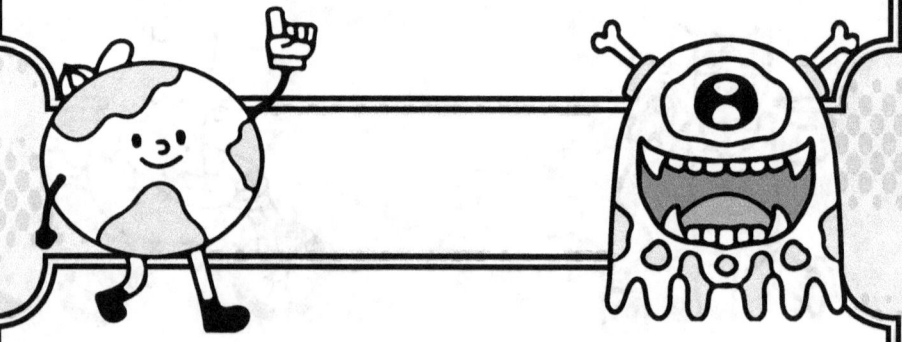

Which mode do cows play in Fortnite?

Cattle Royale.

What does a sheep say to its crush on Valentine's Day?

I really love ewe.

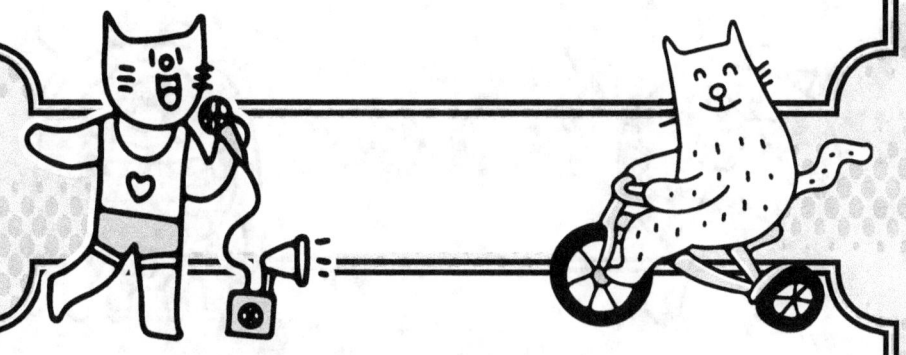

What do you need to make a blueberry cake?

A sad strawberry.

Why do mascara and lipstick never stay mad at each other?

They always make-up.

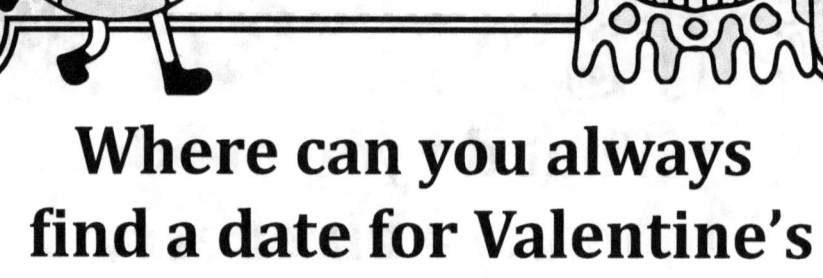

Where can you always find a date for Valentine's Day?

The Calendar.

Where do polar bears cast their votes?

At the North Poll.

How do they make toast in the jungle?

They put it under the Grilla.

I heard the man was furious with the clock...

No, he was just ticked off.

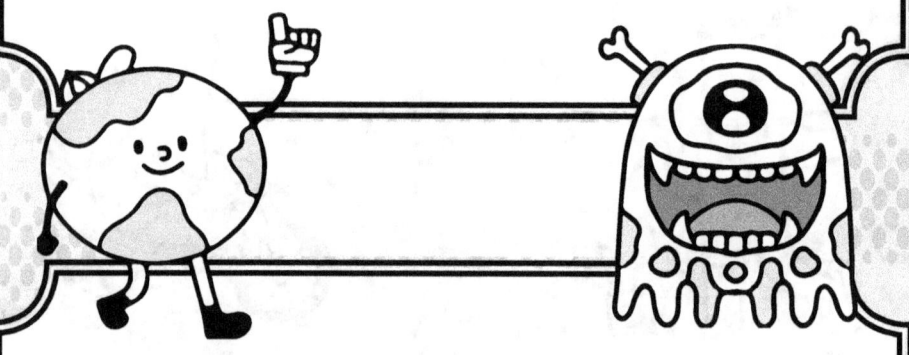

What did the dog say after it sat on the sandpaper?

That's ruff!

What would a lightbulb say to his sweetheart?

I love you a watt.

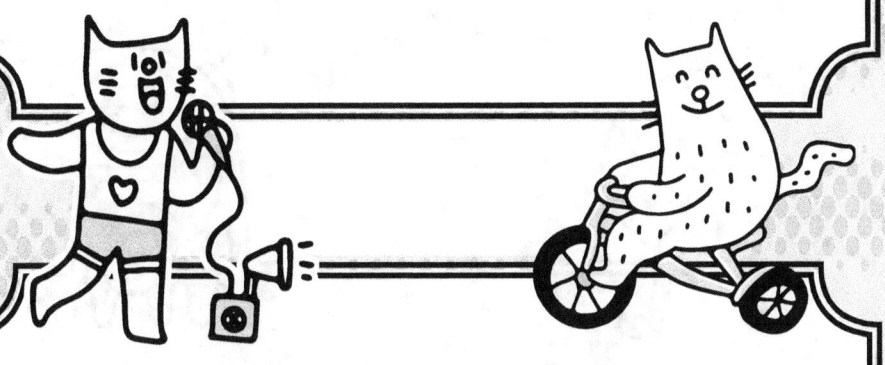

Which type of snake works on a building site?

A boa constructor.

Why does Luke Skywalker never sleep with the lights off?

He is afraid of the Darth.

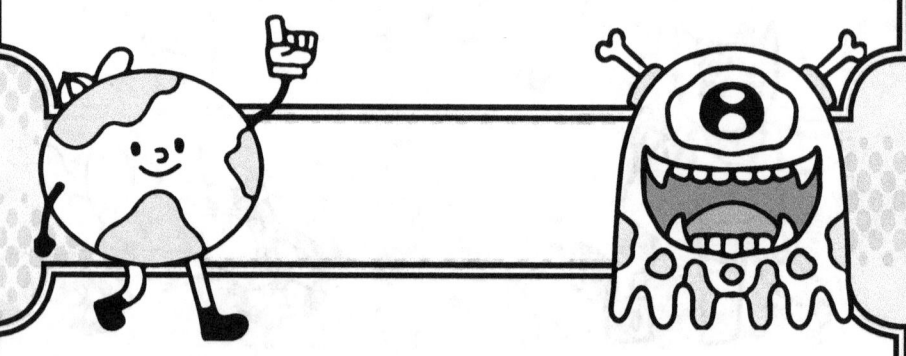

Which kind of dinosaur is good at Fortnite?

A flossoraptor.

What should you get your frog to go on holiday with?

Open toad shoes.

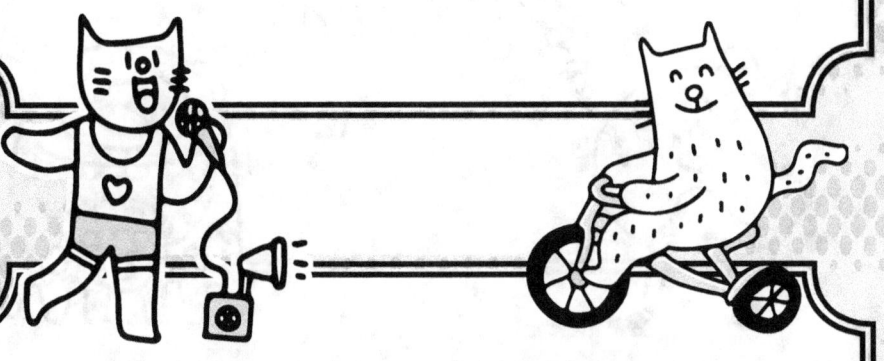

What type of flowers shouldn't you give on Valentine's Day?

Cauliflowers.

Why did the young elephant need a new suitcase before her holiday?

Because all she had was a little trunk.

Knock, knock.
Who's there?
Haven.
Haven who?
Haven you had enough of my knock knock jokes yet?

Why shouldn't you tell jokes while you're ice skating?

In case the cracks up.

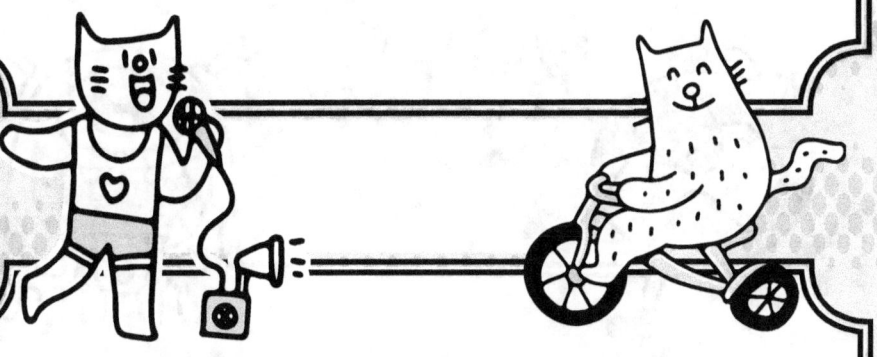

What did the traffic lights scream at the truck?

Don't watch! I'm changing!

What did Venus say to her friend Saturn?

Ring me after school and we'll catch up

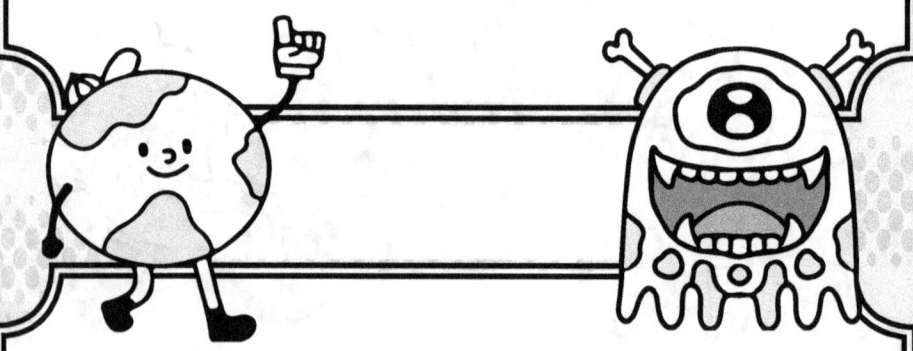

Which snake bakes the best pastries?

A pie-thon.

I am great pals with 25 letters of the alphabet.

But I don't know Y.

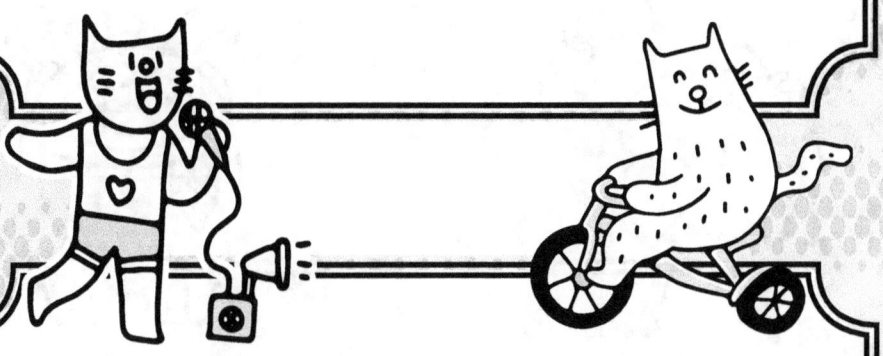

Which fruit do twins love to eat?

Pears.

What begins with P, ends with E and contains lots of letters?

Post Office.

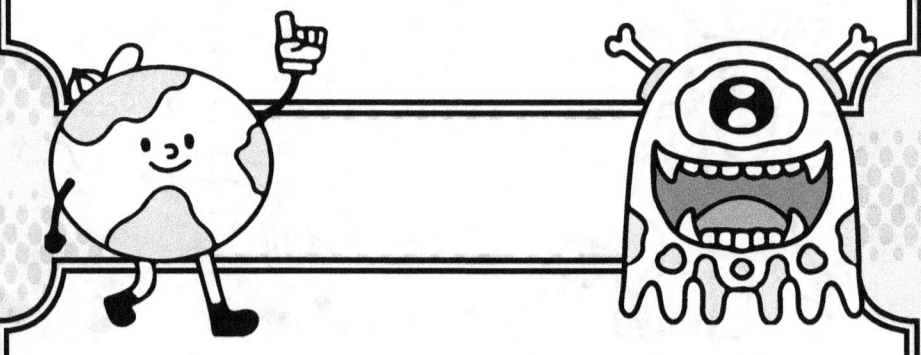

Which area of math do cows love best?

Moo-ltiplication.

Knock, knock.
Who's there?
Kent.
Kent who?
Kent you recognize my voice?

What did Sarabi say to Mufasa when he outran Simba?

You are fit for a King.

What do you call a chicken that tells hilarious jokes?

A comedihen!

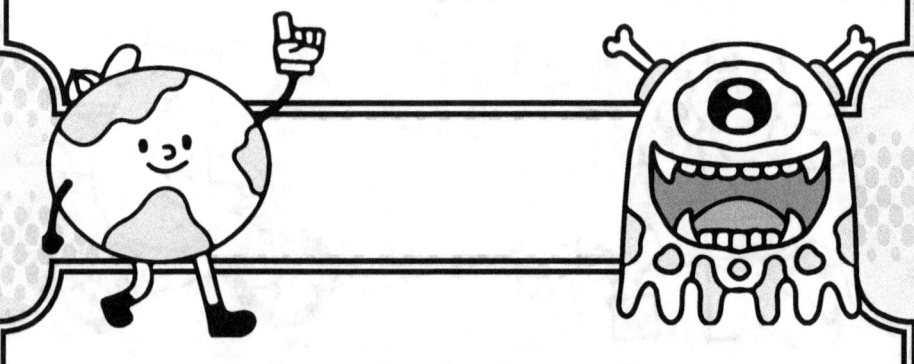

Why did the slug envy the snail?

It was feeling shell-ous.

My brother thought that onions are the only food that can make you cry.

But he also cried when that coconut fell on his head.

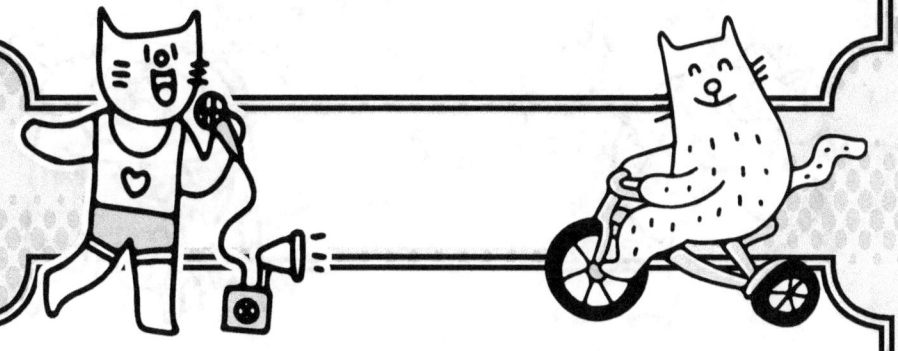

Why did the news reporter interview the ice cream?

She wanted to get the scoop.

What is the name of a girl who stands inside goalposts and catches the ball?

Annette.

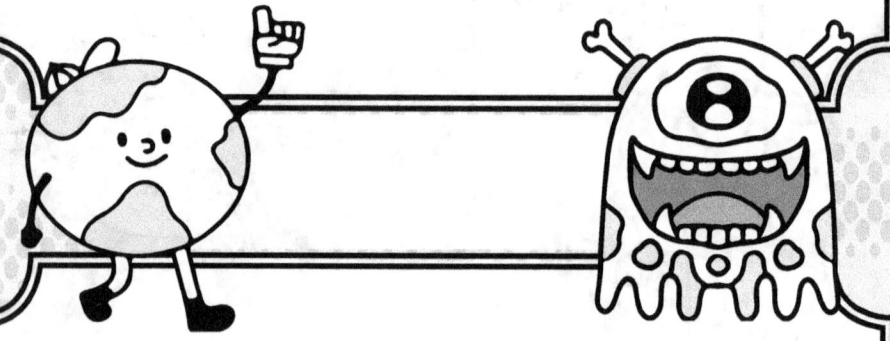

What kind of phones do mermaids use to chat?

Shell phones.

Which type of music concert do geologists love to go to?

Rock concerts.

What made the scientist install a knocker on her door?

She was determined to win the No-bell prize.

www.ingramcontent.com/pod-product-compliance
Lightning Source LLC
Chambersburg PA
CBHW070335120526
44590CB00017B/2892